MASTER-LEVEL BUSINESS & CLIENT DEVELOPMENT ACTIVITY CHECKLISTS

For Lawyers, Law Firms and Other Professional Services Providers

Set 1

JULIE SAVARINO

Published in the United States of America by Julie Savarino, Business Development Inc., www.BusDevInc.com

Publisher's Cataloging-in-Publication Data:
Business Development Inc., Savarino, Julie A.

PRINT ISBN: 978-1-7329-4532-6

EBOOK ISBN: 978-1-7329-4531-9

Library of Congress Control Number: 2018913124

Foreword

THIS BOOK OF CHECKLISTS is an excellent resource. It provides lawyers and other professional services providers with specific, proven, and step-by-step things to do to get the best results from business and client development activities and efforts. Julie Savarino created this book by combining her over thirty years' experience.

Michael Rynowecer, President
The BTI Consulting Group
www.BTIConsulting.com

What Readers Say About This Book

"This book of checklists is a must-read for any lawyer or professional interested in getting the best results from non-billable time they invest in client development, new business development and sales efforts."

—AJ Moss, Member, Dickinson Wright LLP

"This book is a comprehensive yet concise, pragmatic, immediately actionable set of resources. These checklists are a must-have for the desktop or the briefcase of any attorney, business development professional, or legal marketer. Julie Savarino provides context and just the right amount of 'what's-in-it-for-me' to motivate change and growth, leveraging her wealth of experience as a legendary thought leader and coach in the legal marketing field. This book of checklists is invaluable."

—Roy Sexton, Senior Marketing Manager, Clark Hill PLC

"This book is very well-done and useful. Julie Savarino is the master at helping lawyers at all levels maximize their business development potential. Do not go to your next client pitch without the checklists from this book in your back pocket."

—Colin K. Kelly, Partner, Alston & Bird LLP

"What a brilliant idea to develop very practical checklists for business and client development activities! This is not just a guidebook to read; it is a reference manual to use repeatedly, as you navigate everything from responding to RFPs, to engaging in cross-selling or maximizing your results from attending a conference."

—Patrick J. McKenna, Principal, McKenna Associates Inc.

"Similar to the lawyers I work with, I am too busy to do the things I should do, which is why this book is so great. It is broken down by business development activity—from deciding the Go/No-Go of an RFP, to how to make the best use of your time investment in a webinar - all in my favorite format of checklists and numbered lists. Whether you are an attorney sitting at your desk not sure where to start, or a business development professional coaching an attorney on next steps, this book is a great guideline and starting point for what to do next."

—Heather Morse, Director of Marketing
Greenberg Glusker LLP

CHECKLISTS IN THIS BOOK

How to Use the Checklists

In this Book

IF YOU ARE a lawyer, accountant, or other professional services provider, below are three ways to make the best use of the checklists in this book:

- **Overall** – To enhance your overall knowledge, or to refresh it, once you purchase this book, set aside 30 minutes to read/review and mark the checklists and action items relevant to the lawyers/accountants/consultants with whom you work to help develop their book of business.

- **Year-End or New Year Planning** – To support your individual Annual Business or Business Development Plan, use these checklists to ensure each planned activity is optimized to get the best results.

- **When New Opportunities Arise** – Depending on the specific opportunity, refer to the appropriate checklist in this book to be sure to increase your chances of getting the best results from the opportunity and to leverage it.

If you are an in-house marketer/business development coach for a law firm, accounting firm, or other professional services firm, below are four ways to make the best use the checklists in this book:

- **Overall** – To enhance your overall knowledge, or to refresh it, once you purchase this book, set aside 30 minutes to read/review and mark the checklists and action items relevant to the lawyers/accountants/consultants with whom you work to help develop their book of business.

- **Support the Annual Plans and Planning Process** – For Annual Business Plans or Business Development Plans, use these checklists to ensure each planned activity is optimized to get the best results. At the end of the year or the activity, use these checklists to compare what was done and not done, and consider adapting future activities.

- **Use During Individual Coaching Sessions** – When holding a coaching meeting with an individual practitioner, open this book of checklists to review with that practitioner, to be sure the practitioner, you, and your firm are doing everything possible to get the best results from their current and upcoming business development activities.

- **When New Opportunities Arise** – Depending on the specific opportunity, refer to the appropriate checklist in this book to be sure to increase your chances of getting the best results from the opportunity and to leverage it.

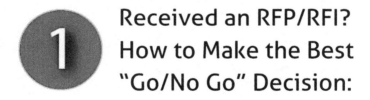 Received an RFP/RFI? How to Make the Best "Go/No Go" Decision:

12 Tips to Maximize the Results from Your Time, Effort, and Investment

☐ **Check conflicts.**

    ☐ Before investing any time whatsoever in reading or responding to a request for proposal (RFP) or a request for information (RFI), immediately request a conflicts check/report on the company, related entities and all persons named in the request.

    ☐ Even if the RFP/RFI was received from an existing client, there may be some level of potential conflict relating to the scope of work or the business as defined in the RFP/RFI.

    ☐ If the RFP/RFI was sent from a potential client (some company or someone for whom you personally or your firm have never done legal work), a conflicts check will also likely show what work (if any) your firm has done for this company/entity in the past, which firm lawyers provided it and, most important, whether there are any existing legal or potential business conflicts.

☐ **Fight your immediate instinct to respond.**

    ☐ Embrace the fact that formal RFPs/RFIs are the most time-intensive but often the least fruitful path to developing significant new business.

    ☐ Many lawyers find that responding to such requests is a waste of time and have stopped participating unless the RFP/RFI comes from a firm client and they need to prevent it from going to another firm.

☐ Having a repeatable process/checklist to respond to RFPs/RFIs is very important because it allows you/your firm to be strategic and efficient, and it may help you/your firm decide not to participate.

☐ If you decide not to participate, send a thoughtfully tailored "thanks, but no thanks" response.

☐ Identify your champion.

☐ Winning an RFP/RFI is often contingent on having a person (internal to the company/entity) who is already or is willing to be a cheerleader/advocate for you/your firm, i.e. someone who already has a strong relationship with you (personally and/or professionally) or a preference for your firm.

☐ If you do not have an "insider" who is willing to give you the lay of the land, including a sense of what is really driving the pitch or RFP/RFI process (e.g., fees, price, politics, personality) and who the decision-makers are, rethink whether you/your firm should participate.

☐ **Read the RFP/RFI in its entirety.**

    ☐ This is especially important if the request came from a company/entity you do not know or know well. At the very least, speed-read the following sections: scope of services, budget/costs, selection criteria, decision-making process and deadlines. Don't forget to mark important information.

    ☐ Identify whether there is a person whose contact information is named in the RFP/RFI. If so, plan to communicate with that person or ask questions prior to submitting your response.

☐ **Take notes.**

    ☐ While carefully reading/reviewing the RFP/RFI, highlight key phrases, requirements and other items. Not having to reread the RFP/RFI will save time when you're preparing your response submission.

    ☐ Better yet, review the RFP/RFI with assistance from your internal or external marketing/business development coach.

☐ **Request assistance.**

    ☐ If your firm has a marketing/business development department, alert the appropriate person(s) in that department about having received the RFP/RFI and ask for their assistance, as desired.

☐ Coordinate internally, to avoid possible communication redundancies and missteps, etc.

☐ Find out whether the firm has received or responded to other RFPs/RFIs for this company/entity in the past and with what results.

☐ Ask for a firmwide check on "who knows whom" at this company/entity and what insights your colleagues may have.

☐ Prepare a response format that puts the firm in the best light.

☐ **Assess the value of the opportunity.**

☐ Determine whether the (usually considerable) time and effort needed to draft and prepare a response to this RFP/RFI is a good use of your/the firm's time. Establish "qualification criteria" based on the information in the RFP/RFI document and anything else you know or have learned about the organization.

☐ Qualification criteria answer the question, "Is this a strong/ desirable opportunity?", such as:

☐ Is this a client I want (or my firm wants)?

☐ Does the organization pay promptly?

- ☐ Is it well-funded, insured and/or indemnified?
- ☐ Does it operate in a desirable industry?
- ☐ Is the organization viable in terms of size and/or stage of development?
- ☐ Does our firm excel at the type and scope of work described in the RFP/RFI?
- ☐ Can we pitch and do/deliver this work profitably?
- ☐ Can we establish a one-to-one personal relationship with one or more buyers/decision-makers/influencers prior to submitting the RFP/RFI response?
- ☐ What other qualification/selection criteria are unique to this firm/client/situation?

☐ **Ask yourself: is this an offensive or defensive opportunity?**

- ☐ Determine whether the scope of services as defined in the RFP/RFI is the type of work you already do for the client, or whether it is a new or seldom-provided service.

  - ☐ If it is the type of work you already do/have done for the client, is this RFP/RFI a "defensive" opportunity (i.e., are they trying to reduce fees, or reduce the number of outside firms/lawyers they use, etc.)?

☐ Or is it an "offensive" opportunity (i.e., is there an opportunity to expand on work previously done or other types of work you have not done)?

☐ Whether the RFP/RFI is a defensive or an offensive opportunity will likely change your response strategy, decisions, amount of time and money invested and/or next steps.

☐ If the RFP/RFI was received from an existing client:

  ☐ What person and department/division within the existing client/company/entity sent the RFP/RFI, signed the letter or sent the email?

  ☐ Do you personally (or does someone in your firm) know that individual?

  ☐ Who else from the company/entity is named or listed in the RFP/RFI, and who at your firm knows those individuals?

☐ **Determine origin.**

  ☐ Other than for public entities who are required to send RFPs/RFIs, if you were not aware that the RFP/RFI was being sent before you received it, is there an explanation within the document itself as to why the company/entity sent the RFP/RFI?

☐ Is there a section in the RFP/RFI that discusses the company's/entity's goals, objectives or desired results from this RFP/RFI and process?

☐ Consider who else in your firm may work or may have worked with this client and ask whether those individuals were aware or had advance notice that this RFP/RFI was being sent.

☐ If you have never received an RFP/RFI from this company/entity before, determine how you/your firm got on their list.

☐ **Ask to meet in person.**

☐ If this company/entity is a highly qualified client/potential client, or if you decide that the RFP/RFI may be a good opportunity and use of your time, offer (either by email or by phone) an in-person meeting on a complimentary basis prior to submitting your response.

☐ If the company/entity representative agrees to answer your preliminary questions before you prepare your response, plan carefully. This step is one of the most important in the RFP/RFI process! Think of it as a "pre-response interview/meeting," and plan to ask all the questions you would want answered in a post-response interview if you did not win the RFP/RFI.

☐ If the person says no or will not communicate directly with you (by phone, by email or in person) before you send in your response, the chances that you/your firm will win the RFP/RFI are less than 30%.

☐ **Prepare for face time.**

    ☐ Prepare for this "pre-response interview/ meeting" very carefully and thoroughly.

        ☐ Face-to-face contact is how at least 70% of final decisions are made (not necessarily at that exact time, but more often later).

        ☐ Research each person who will be at the meeting. Learn their background (where they went to school, interests, etc.) and seek out commonalities.

        ☐ Consider diversity, backgrounds and personal styles of the representatives from the client/entity and also from the firm. Match and balance as needed.

☐ **Plan to ask key questions.**

    ☐ Make it clear that all answers have one purpose: for you/your firm to provide an RFP/RFI response that will best meet the needs of the client/entity.

    ☐ Plan to ask and have someone take copious notes on responses to your questions.

☐ Prepare and ask such questions as:

    ☐ What drove the decision to send this RFP/RFI?

    ☐ Was it sent due to internal executive or staffing changes ... or in an effort to control outside legal spend?

    ☐ Was it intended to improve diversity ... or to improve the quality of results or representation, and/or the services provided in conjunction with the representation?

    ☐ Are there any other reasons the RFP/RFI was sent?

    ☐ What does success look like for the client?

    ☐ How important is budget/total cost to the client?

    ☐ Does the client have any budget/cost estimate in mind?

    ☐ Is the client interested in AFAs (alternative fee arrangements)?

    ☐ What is the decision-making process (if that is not spelled out in the RFP/RFI document)?

    ☐ Who will be making the final decision, and when?

2 Have a New Business "Pitch" Meeting Coming Up?

21 Proven Tips on Ways to Win

THIS CHECKLIST ASSUMES you know and are well-versed in the substance related to the pitch (i.e., the ins and outs of the services/solutions you are proposing). So instead, this checklist emphasizes form, techniques, packaging and process tips to help you win business.

☐ **Schedule time to prepare.**

> ☐ Winning any pitch, like planning the pitch process itself, is part science and part art. This checklist provides key tips relating to the science of winning new business, which takes time, effort and discipline.

☐ **Prior Preparation Prevents Poor Performance (the 5 Ps).**

> ☐ Approximately 80% of winning any pitch for legal or other professional services is attributed to thorough preparation, research, the pre-pitch interview, coordination, practice, rehearsal and follow-up.

> ☐ Only about 20% of winning is attributable to the substance that is discussed during the pitch itself, yet most lawyers and other professionals spend most of their time planning and creating materials and slides for the substance of the presentation. Do not make that mistake!

☐ **Do some homework and analyze it.**

    ☐ If you have marketing/business development staff at your firm, ask them to assist you in this process. If not, consider hiring an outside client development coach.

    ☐ When the experience and competency levels of lawyers/firms are similar (as they often are, at least from the client's perspective), the vast majority of pitches are won based on personal chemistry. So learn all you can about each key client/potential client and contact person before you contact or pitch to them.

    ☐ Learn everything there is to know about the company, especially the latest news and trends.

    ☐ Compile all legal work done in the past for similar or related companies, and range of what they paid.

☐ **Identify and communicate with your champion.**

    ☐ Winning a pitch is often contingent on having an internal client cheerleader/advocate within the client company/entity – someone who already has a strong personal and/or professional relationship with you/your firm, or a preference for you/your firm.

    ☐ If you do not have an "insider" who is willing to give you the lay of the land, describe the relevant personalities ahead of time, and offer you a sense of what is really driving the pitch/RFP/RFI process (e.g., fees, price, politics, personality, their desire for AFAs (Alternative Fee Arrangements)), rethink whether you/your firm should participate, and if so, to what degree of effort and investment.

☐ **Request a meeting or call.**

☐ If you have not already done so and are not barred by the language in an RFP/pitch document, ask for and conduct a "pre-pitch interview" meeting with an appropriate representative from the company/entity.

☐ If the pitch represents a high-priority opportunity, try to meet with the representative in person. If an in-person meeting is not possible, talk by phone or video conference.

☐ Review and analyze the information described above and use it to prepare well-conceived and well-researched questions that can help you/your firm put your "best foot forward."

☐ Do not ask questions that are already answered in the RFP/RFI document itself, or questions that focus on information you plan to include in your written response.

☐ Instead, ask questions such as:

- ☐ What exactly would you like to know, and what do you expect, so I can be as helpful and useful to you as possible during our pitch meeting?
- ☐ What are the most important priorities, concerns, or issues that you would like to hear about or discuss first?
- ☐ Is there any background information (that is not contained in the RFP/pitch document or request) that would be helpful for us to know in advance of preparing?
- ☐ Is there an estimated budget, fee range and/or targets you can share with us?
- ☐ Who (if anyone) are you currently using for this work, and what would you like done differently/improved?
- ☐ What is your level of effort and risk on the matters covered by the RFP?
- ☐ What are your ideal and most probable expected outcomes?

☐ **Analyze the audience.**

- ☐ Ask yourself or the client/prospect the following people and process centric questions (if you do not know the answers already):
  - ☐ Who will be attending the pitch meeting, and what are their roles in the decision-making process?

- ☐ Do we have an internal champion/advocate?
- ☐ Will the final decision-makers be there?
- ☐ Are any of the attendees' influencers but not necessarily decision-makers?
- ☐ Are the attendees prepared to act/decide on the spot? If not, what is their decision-making process?
- ☐ What is their budget (both low and high ends)?
- ☐ What are they asking for, what do they need and want, and are those in alignment?
- ☐ What is their current level of knowledge about me/my firm?

☐ **Define your strategy.**

- ☐ Consider all the above (and more) to craft your pitch strategy (i.e., determine a path/steps for what to win and how), which often consists of answering these questions:

  - ☐ Is this a "pitch to win" situation or a "pitch to initiate a relationship" situation? Or is it simply a pitch for practice? Or is it more than one of these alternatives?
  - ☐ How likely are we to win?
  - ☐ Is it a no-holds-barred, full-court press pitch, just the basics, or somewhere in between?

☐ Who should be involved and in what role?

☐ How will we price/bill? Do the firm's billing or conflicts committees need to be alerted or involved?

☐ What makes us different or better? What is our unique selling proposition?

☐ What value or features can and should we offer, over and above those of any other firm?

☐ How will we advance this pitch to a buying decision?

☐ How will we follow up if we win? If we do not? Who will stay in touch? How and when?

☐ What other strategic considerations are relevant to this client/pitch/situation?

☐ **Plan your use of time.**

☐ Consider and plan your use of the allocated pitch time very carefully.

☐ If you have been allocated one hour for the pitch, do not make the common mistake of filling the entire hour going over PowerPoint® slides that center around your firm, your experience and you.

☐ Instead, use the winning formula of planning to present only a maximum of 20-30 minutes on prepared/formal remarks, and the rest of the time, ask for questions or raise commonly asked questions.

☐ Plan to use the rest of the time to communicate one-to-one with the attendees, asking insightful questions to get to the root of the issue, their business and personal motivations, preferences, etc.

☐ So, ahead of time, prepare at least five key, well-conceived questions to ask the attendees/potential clients.

☐ **Anticipate and plan lots of questions.**

☐ The 80/20 Rule is proven to win pitches: For 80% of the time, you should be asking questions and/or engaging in meaningful dialogue with the attendees/potential clients, and for only 20% of the time, you should be talking about yourself, your firm and your experience.

☐ **Organize carefully.**

☐ Package/script your pitch completely from beginning to end.

☐ Define who will introduce and lead the pitch, and how.

☐ Plan transition statements from one speaker or topic to the next.

☐ Identify relevant yet brief stories to weave into your remarks.

☐ Decide how to make them relevant to the audience/attendees.

☐ Determine who will summarize next steps and close.

☐ **Check your demeanor.**

☐ Before pitching, take a minute to reflect internally on your current mind-set, disposition and thinking.

☐ If you are irritated, angry or anxious in any way, you need to let that go and focus on the task at hand.

☐ The most effective thing you can do to prepare to win a pitch is to be as professional, courteous, helpful, kind and gracious as possible to everyone (including the janitors, secretaries and any other staff people involved) throughout the pitch process.

☐ "Personal chemistry" (i.e., whether the client/prospective client actually likes or meshes with you), is the single criterion that can influence at least 70% of the decision about whether to hire you, your colleagues or your firm.

☐ Avoid making assumptions or presumptions.

☐ **Be confident yet humble.**

   ☐ A key element of any successful pitch is to demonstrate not only knowledge and experience but also passion, commitment, enthusiasm and energy.

   ☐ Be very aware of your personal style and how you could be perceived. Be confident yet not arrogant.

   ☐ Smile, be pleasant and manage your emotions.

☐ **Rehearse.**

   ☐ Rehearse at least once.

   ☐ Studies show that the vast majority of winning pitches were practiced or rehearsed, and then improved/tweaked at least twice.

   ☐ Unfortunately, most lawyers and other professionals do not have/make the time to practice. Instead, they mostly "wing it," which is a recipe for failure.

☐ **Remember that what's in it for the client is what matters most.**

   ☐ On pitch day, remember, it is <u>not</u> all about you.

   ☐ It <u>is</u> all about the client, their case or problem, and providing the best possible options to resolve or handle it.

☐ They would not have invited you if they did not already think you were qualified and capable of doing the work.

☐ Strive to leave them with something helpful and useful, or something they did not know before they met you.

☐ **Turn off your cell phone and put in in your pocket or purse.**

☐ Make sure you have turned off your cell phone and all other mobile devices, and do not pull them out for any reason whatsoever – unless they ask you to.

☐ **Avoid slouching.**

☐ Watch your posture, and do not look at your notes or otherwise look away when someone else is presenting or talking.

☐ **Demonstrate sincere interest and concern.**

☐ If you took time to prepare/do homework, let them know you did so on a nonbillable basis.

☐ Make and maintain eye contact.

☐ During the pitch, weave in questions often.

☐ Demonstrate through what you say that you are prepared and have a decent understanding of their issues, and then provide possible solutions and alternatives.

☐ Take the time to engage those present, not speak at them.

☐ If you are formally presenting using slides, do not face toward and speak to the screen.

☐ Suggest options.

☐ Make sure to include simple AFA (alternative fee arrangement) options and a list of value-added and/or complimentary services or features you/your firm are willing to offer.

☐ Summarize at the end.

☐ At the end of the pitch, make sure to summarize the key services, features and benefits you covered, and state (if you have not done so during the pitch) that you are able and ready, and you sincerely desire, to represent them and/or help them meet their goals and objectives.

☐ Verbally suggest next steps.

☐ Plan your closing remarks ahead of time and make it a "tight-forward motion" close. For example, enthusiastically say something like the following: "We very much appreciate your taking the time to meet with us. We sincerely hope we provided you with information, resources and options that will prove helpful and useful to you with this issue or in the future. What else can we do or provide to demonstrate how much we could help if retained?"

☐ At this point, if the following has not already been covered, ask: "What is the next step? When do you anticipate making your decision? Would you like us to get back in touch with you later this week or next week?"

☐ As a final point, as appropriate ask whether they would like to be added to relevant firm email alert lists, and offer to send them an opt-in link or tell them you will add them.

☐ **Coordinate internally after the pitch.**

☐ Once the pitch is over, debrief with your pitch team to assess what went well and what could be done differently or improved next time.

☐ Ask about and coordinate all follow-up communications so that any thank-you notes, etc., are signed by all firm members who pitched.

☐ Plan ahead to avoid having every person who attended send their own follow-up individually, which can (and does) annoy clients and make them think the firm does not coordinate or streamline communications and outreach.

3 Meeting With a Prospective Client?

8 Tips to Maximize the Results From Any One-on-One or Small-Group Sales Meeting

☐ **Clear conflicts.**

    ☐ Make sure you have checked and cleared all conflicts – both legal and any potential business conflicts.

☐ **Do some homework.**

    ☐ At least 30 minutes before departing for the meeting, Google the person/people you are meeting (even if you know them well).

    ☐ Google the company/entity where the person/contacts work. On the company website, visit "News" to see what has happened at the company during the past several months or is currently happening.

    ☐ Visit their LinkedIn and other relevant web pages to see what is new. Learn where they went to school and whom they know; look for commonalities and similar interests.

    ☐ Search for the individual name and company name in Westlaw, LexisNexis, PACER or Courthouse News to get a basic snapshot of any legal matters or issues, especially if the person you are meeting is a client and/or a potential referral source. For an existing client, run all cases or matters since the last date you saw or communicated with them.

☐ **Prepare good questions.**

    ☐ Use the information gained from the above to prepare in your mind (or in notes) a few questions about the person you will meet and their world.

    ☐ Be ready to ask your questions during the meeting as appropriate, using the flow of conversation as a guide.

☐ **Load your mobile.**

    ☐ Make sure you have the right contact information in your mobile phone, in case you run into traffic, are running late, etc.

☐ **Be on time.**

    ☐ Being late for any meeting signals a lack of professionalism, discipline and respect.

☐ **Act like a host rather than a guest.**

    ☐ Greet the person confidently when they arrive – stand up, smile, extend your hand, professionally and firmly shake their hand, and introduce yourself.

☐ **Start with pleasantries.**

    ☐ Ask a basic question like "How are you?" and really pay attention/listen to their response.

☐ If they are at your office, be helpful – ask, "Can I get you something to drink?" or "Can I take your coat?" If you know them already, ask something like "How was the drive/commute?" "How is/are ____ [spouse/friend/children] doing?" etc.

☐ Be sure to start the meeting by focusing for three to ten minutes on pleasantries/common courtesies/social issues.

☐ Ask questions about the person: "How is your family?" or "How is work going?"

☐ Then turn the discussion to business by saying something like "Shall we get to work?"

☐ **Take notes.**

☐ You or someone on your team should take careful notes during the meeting (or immediately after).

☐ If the meeting is with a potential new client, ask for permission before you begin writing, and let the client know that everything discussed will remain confidential.

☐ Use the "split" technique to take notes: Write all personal/social details you may have learned on the top or side of the page, and write all the material of substance below it.

☐ After the meeting, store in the person's Outlook contact record all useful information, such as children's names, spouse's name, where he/she went to school, personal preferences/likes, etc.

☐ Obviously, also use your notes to act upon the substance of the meeting (e.g., find and send an article, draft a document, delegate tasks).

5 Keys to Effective Cross-Servicing/Cross-Selling

☐ **Be aware that change is *constant*.** "Business as usual" is rarely predictable or consistent.

☐ At *least* every 12 to 18 months, your clients face new and vexing problems. These issues change like clockwork. Some will appear, disappear and reappear over time, but the issues will always have new and more complex twists.

☐ This does not even include the unexpected fires, crises, lawsuits filed – all situations that can arise on any day and that have legal or other business ramifications requiring outside legal or other professional assistance/advice.

☐ **Note the prime cross-selling times.**

☐ Approximately two to three or four months before or after calendar/fiscal year-end is a prime cross-selling time.

☐ For companies/organizations on a calendar year-end schedule, the best cross-selling/cross-service times are around October/November and January/February/March.

☐ **Use PROACTIVE routines and habits.**

☐ If you do not already incorporate the routine of conducting a close of matter/case discussion with each client, create that habit. Every corporate client is also an individual who may have estate, family law, and tax issues or needs. *Every* client is a potential referral source.

☐ If you do not already have the habit of scheduling (at least annually) a non-billable, face-to-face meeting with key clients, to ask what's new, what's developing, what keeps them up at night and other high-value questions, create that routine now.

☐ Develop a system or routine for you, your firm's marketing staff or colleagues in your firm to regularly do research, track changes and developments, and update you/your team.

☐ Create a system or method to track and identify new and developing issues by geography, industry, client, and type of problem.

☐ Make an effort to ask your clients whether they are experiencing any of these issues, before they start seeking solutions or answers without you.

☐ **Consider and evaluate the following factors regarding cross-servicing opportunities:**

☐ Does the person or company have a need for legal services?

☐ Is the issue/matter of strategic importance or routine to the person/company?

☐ Is the company familiar with me and/or our firm?

☐ Is there an incumbent firm providing the services?

☐ Has the relationship with the company been in place long and expanded over time?

☐ Do we know or can we reach the relevant decision-makers and/or be introduced to them?

☐ Raise the most current, vexing issues and problems that companies/organizations face, such as:

☐ The changes in the current regulatory framework/laws in the United States, Europe and other regions/countries.

☐ A range of post-BREXIT issues and what the impact will be on global companies.

☐ Cybersecurity, privacy, and data breaches, and the daunting task of keeping up with relevant changes in global, national, and state rules and regulations.

☐ Identifying, managing and mitigating risk.

☐ Risk comes in many forms, all of which entail assessing probabilities of the unknown.

☐ Work to identify the most important risks your key clients face, by type. Then work with others in your firm to compile a list of ways to mitigate, options and/or possible solutions.

☐ Schedule a face-to-face meeting to discuss these concerns with your clients in a private setting, where your discussion cannot be overheard.

☐ Any of the many other issues that exist and are unique to your clients, but that are discovered only by asking the right questions.

5 Attending a Conference or Seminar?

12 Tips to Maximize Your Results from Attending

☐ **Define your purpose/objective for attending.**

  ☐ Ask yourself what your primary and secondary purposes are for attending.

- [ ] To gain continuing education?
- [ ] To network?
- [ ] Both?

- [ ] Gaining continuing education *and* networking are often the two main purposes for attending a conference/seminar.

- [ ] Create a plan of action ahead of time to ensure you will attain your objective(s) by attending. Specific suggestions are below.

[ ] Prepare immediately.

- [ ] Mark, star or circle on the agenda, at the time you register, the sessions of greatest interest to you.

- [ ] Also mark the speakers whom you are most interested in hearing and/or meeting.

[ ] Connect with the person in charge of the event.

- [ ] Look up the person(s) in charge of the event. Obtain their phone number(s), and mark on your calendar a reminder to call one month before the event to ask whether they would please send you a copy of the attendance list by name and company only (unless you are a paid sponsor of the event, it is best not to ask for attendees' contact information).

- [ ] Let the organizer(s) know that having this list will help you maximize your time spent at the event. Experience shows they will send it to you 80% of the time.

☐ **Use social media and create social media posts ahead of time.**

☐ When you register, post on LinkedIn and other relevant places that you plan to attend the event, and ask your friends and connections to let you know whether they plan to attend.

☐ Write tailored posts, "tag" the event producers or organizers, and add relevant hashtags.

☐ If there is not already a dedicated, custom app for the event or a LinkedIn or Facebook group for attendees of the event, consider creating a private group on a relevant social media platform and let the event producers know you did so, in case they are aware of others who may want to join.

☐ **Plan your trip to maximize opportunities.**

☐ Do not book travel until you know whether you can add an extra day or add on a breakfast, lunch, coffee and dinner into your schedule when there.

☐ To maximize client development opportunities, it is best to plan a few hours or a half day upon arrival and before departure so that you can schedule additional meetings.

    ☐ Go to your LinkedIn account and click "My Network" on the upper toolbar; then your connections then "Search with Filters" select "Location" and scroll to/select the location or add an additional location filter, if necessary, for where the conference/seminar will be held.

    ☐ You will be shown all your connections who live or work in that area.

    ☐ Consider whether you want to visit any of these connections while there. If so, reach out to them.

    ☐ Take a minute to check LinkedIn for secondary connections to whom you might want to be introduced, and ask whether your connections would be willing to set up an introduction over breakfast/coffee, etc.

☐ **Create a schedule.**

    ☐ Do not just "show up" or "play it by ear" when you arrive.

    ☐ Instead, plan ahead and create a schedule with notes to yourself on what you plan to discuss/raise (both pleasantries and substance) at each meeting you have scheduled.

    ☐ Plan how you will introduce yourself to those at the conference whom you do not yet know.

☐ **Create a better response.**

    ☐ How should you respond when someone asks: "What do you do?" Avoid saying the usual: "I'm a lawyer" or "I'm an accountant."

    ☐ Instead, if you are a commercial litigator, say something like "I help companies resolve major problems."

    ☐ Or if you are a transactional lawyer, respond by saying something like "I help get business deals closed in CITY/AREA."

    ☐ These kinds of responses are different and invite inquiry and discussion.

☐ **Pack business cards.**

    ☐ Bring plenty of business cards with you.

    ☐ Have your LinkedIn profile ready to send.

    ☐ Have your vCard ready on your mobile device and know exactly how to beam/send it.

    ☐ If there is a custom app for the event, make sure to download it ahead of time.

    ☐ If appropriate, you may also want to create a "Quick Response" (QR) code, which is a barcode you can store on your mobile device that contains your contact information or other information of interest that you may want to share with those you meet.

☐ **Arrive early and stay late.**

☐ Try to arrive 5 to 10 minutes early and/or stay late for every session and meal during the event (as your schedule allows).

☐ Often it is possible to meet interesting people and make valuable connections when lingering outside the meeting rooms or taking a seat at a lunch/dinner table filled with people you do not know.

☐ Similarly, if you want to meet the speakers, decide to arrive early before their session (because they will often be present to prep), or stay after the session and introduce yourself then.

☐ **Make time at the end of every day to take notes.**

☐ Regularly take notes on whom you met, what you discussed, and how and when you plan to follow up.

☐ Without this commitment and effort, it is very unlikely that your networking will bear fruit.

☐ Take notes on your mobile device or on the backs of business cards, etc.

☐ **Send a tailored LinkedIn connection request to everyone you meet.**

    ☐ Do not send the default "I'd like to add you to my LinkedIn network"; instead, personalize it.

☐ **Set Outlook auto-reminders.**

    ☐ Set a reminder for two to four weeks after the conference, so you can follow up by sending thank-you notes, emails, LinkedIn connection requests, etc. Consider sending summaries of what you learned and relevant content/articles, etc., to those you met, know or to people in your other professional circles.

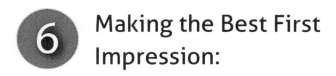 Making the Best First
Impression:

16 Tips for an Effective
Introductory Speech (commonly
known as an "Elevator Pitch")

☐ **Develop a personalized elevator pitch (EP).**

    ☐ Your elevator speech pitch (EP) is defined as a short, verbal summary using words/phrases that quickly and simply define you, your service or firm, and your/its value.

    ☐ Your words should describe the value from the client's perspective, not from yours as a lawyer or other professional.

☐ **Use your EP to network.**

    ☐ Your EP should be used whenever you are in a situation where you can meet or network with people you do not yet know as appropriate, such as:

        ☐ While waiting in line at a coffee shop,

        ☐ While waiting in line for tickets,

        ☐ When seated on a train or plane, or

        ☐ When attending an event, conference, party, seminar, etc.

    ☐ An EP can be used anywhere there are unfamiliar faces.

☐ **Use your EP for various purposes.**

    ☐ To introduce yourself in a memorable way, initiate rapport, and make you favorably stand out from or appear different from other lawyers or professionals.

☐ To spark the listener's interest by saying something memorable – something that spurs questions and a conversation.

☐ To invite a conversation that creates "leads" or opportunities for new business or referrals.

☐ Welcome the chance to engage in a conversation and be prepared to initiate one.

☐ **Remember the #1 purpose of an EP.**

☐ The main purpose of an EP, encompassing all of the above, is to create dialogue/conversation with another person – not to simply answer a question.

☐ **Have an EP ready for various situations.**

☐ You never know when you can initiate and engage in conversations that can be useful to you now or in the future.

☐ You *never know* whom you might meet, whom they know/are related to, or what they might be able to do to help your career or clients.

☐ Here is a recent example: A lawyer well-versed in initiating conversations started talking to a man in line behind him at a coffee shop. As it turned out, the man owned a distribution company, and eventually the lawyer was able to introduce the man to a person he knew, and the two ended up entering into a supplier relationship. Since the lawyer introduced them, the man the lawyer met while in line at the coffee shop hired the lawyer's firm to draft and complete the contract.

☐ **Let your EP address the commonly asked question "What do you do?" – but in a more interesting way.**

    ☐ Do not make the typical mistake of responding by saying, "I am a lawyer," "I am a litigator," "I am a commercial litigator", "I am an accountant", and so on.

    ☐ These labels and phrases are meaningless to most people and are too technical and generic to make you memorable or distinctive in the mind of the listener.

    ☐ Plus, they do very little to pique a listener's interest or start a productive, positive conversation.

☐ **Know how long an EP should be.**

    ☐ Your EP should be delivered in the time it takes to complete an elevator ride – 20 seconds to, at the most, 2 minutes.

    ☐ You should have several variations of your EP prepared, memorized and ready to communicate in various situations.

☐ You should have a 20-second EP, a 2-minute EP and a 20-minute EP ready to go, for internal use (within your firm) and externally (for potential clients, referral sources and others).

Internal Examples:

☐ "I am in the tax practice group in Boston, but I focus on tax controversies and litigation. Do you know of any firm clients that may be facing such issues?"

☐ "I was working on managing e-discovery for the X wage and hour case, but now that it is wrapping up, I have more time available. Anything I can help you with?"

External Examples:

☐ "I counsel banks and credit unions on the legal issues they face."

☐ "I represent manufacturers when they have legal problems."

☐ "I help businesses grow and make money by putting deals together."

☐ "I work on complex legal cases, such as when [explain a recent, high-profile case that your firm – not necessarily you – handled, or an example from recent headlines]."

☐ "I work with privately owned businesses to help them resolve employment problems."

☐ "I help protect inventions and help inventors make more money from them."

☐ You should have at the ready one or two specific examples you can describe. Only use examples that are non-confidential and/or are non-attributed generalizations about any firm client.

☐ **Know your firm, the latest news and happenings, and what's new or hot.**

☐ One of the best 20-second EPs to have ready addresses the hottest, most prominent, most publicly known cases or matters your firm is working on. Be prepared to say, "I work at Smith & Smith law firm. We were involved in the recent case you may have read about or seen on TV, involving _____."

☐ Notice the use of "we."

☐ When asked what you do, you need not respond with an exact answer about yourself; you can start by describing your firm's or one of your partner's recent activities/results.

☐ **Know some relevant details.**

☐ You MUST know some interesting info about that case/matter you've chosen to discuss, because the listener will ask you such questions as:

- ☐ "How did that come about?"
- ☐ "What happened in the end?"
- ☐ "What's happening with that case now?"

☐ Remember, the whole point of an EP is to start a conversation and engage in meaningful dialogue with the listener.

☐ **Be prepared to ask about and/or share personal or professional interests.**

- ☐ You can ask something like:
  - ☐ "What made you decide to attend this conference?"
  - ☐ "Are you a member of this association?"
  - ☐ "Is your child playing today?"
  - ☐ "Are you a donor?"

☐ **Have a generic EP at the ready.**

- ☐ Have at least one generic response you can always use.
  - ☐ For example, to answer the question "What do you do?", I often reply, "I make lawyers richer." That typically elicits a chuckle, and a response like "How do you do that?"

☐ This gives me the perfect segue into anything else I may want to mention, raise, or emphasize.

☐ **Consider appropriate context.**

☐ "Context" means knowing a bit about the person with whom you are communicating, which will allow you to tailor your response to them.

☐ Ideally, you are not caught off guard without any context when you answer the question "What do you do?"

☐ For example, perhaps you meet a person on a plane who says she is an engineer. You could say:

☐ "What type of engineer are you?"

☐ "Where do you work?" or

☐ "Our firm works with engineers to help protect their inventions and to help them make money."

☐ This response entices a question in response, such as "Really? How so?" Congratulations, you have now started a conversation, which is the first step in making a contact and establishing rapport.

☐ So, talk less, listen more and ask the other person questions.

☐ **Consider using a question in your response, speech or pitch.**

    ☐ Ask a question such as "Do you have insurance?" or "Have you ever had a problem with an employee?" If the response is yes, you can say something like "I help insurance companies settle and pay for ____ claims" or "I help employers resolve sticky situations with employees."

    ☐ Be ready to state your firm's name, something memorable about your firm (such as "You may have heard of our firm; we represented X in a high-profile case") and what you personally do (such as "I provide legal counsel and advice to businesses of all types in the _____ area/industry" or "I help companies avoid sticky legal problems").

    ☐ To describe the firm and yourself, be ready with a few non-attributed examples.

☐ **Rehearse your EP.**

    ☐ To be comfortable and confident, you must practice your EP.

    ☐ First, do so out loud and only to yourself, perhaps while driving or exercising. Notice how your words flow.

☐ Do they contain something of interest to the listener?

☐ Do they convey professionalism and enthusiasm for what you do and where you work?

☐ If you get hung up on any words or phrases, consider recrafting them.

☐ Practice until your EP sounds natural and your comfort level increases.

☐ Then practice with your significant other, spouse or best friend, and ask for their feedback/suggestions.

☐ Continue to practice at sporting events, in airports, on airplanes and at events.

☐ You will likely refine and tweak your EP many times over the course of your career.

☐ **Be aware of how you use your voice.**

☐ When speaking, remember to emphasize key points and/or phrases using volume, inflection and/or change of pace. For example, the words underlined in this example could be emphasized when speaking: "I'm an attorney who works just as hard to <u>keep my clients out of court</u>."

☐ Make sure to use a downward inflection at the end of sentences to make your statements more definitive, confident and persuasive.

☐ If you have never used a professional presentation coach, consider hiring one.

☐ **Capture new people you meet and what you discussed.**

☐ Develop a process to "capture" (formally keep track of) everyone you meet. Do not rely on your memory.

☐ Ask for each individual's business card (or Google the person) so you can put their information into your Outlook contacts, recording where you met them in the "Notes" area.

☐ You never know when someone you meet may be of help to you (or to those you know) in the future!

7 Speaking at a Seminar or Conference?

8 Tips to Maximize the Results from Your Speaking Engagement

☐ **Start preparing as soon as you accept the speaking invitation.**

☐ Once you have accepted a speaking engagement, alert your in-house marketing staff and assistant, and request their assistance.

☐ Once you have received the email, letter or phone call confirming your speaking engagement, review the speaker guidelines carefully, and make note of key deadlines and required deliverables.

☐ Schedule appointments with yourself in your Outlook now for at least two weeks ahead of all due dates; a week or two ahead of your appearance, to request the attendance list (by name and company, if the point person does not want to send you the complete contact info); the day before the speech (to practice, at least once); and two to three weeks after the speech, to follow up with those you met and to send thank-you notes to the entity/person who invited, booked or assisted you. You may prefer to ask your assistant to create these Outlook appointments for you.

☐ Send a connection request on LinkedIn and make an Outlook contact for the point person who invited you to speak.

☐ Place a call to introduce yourself to the point person, thank them, and ask any specific questions you may have after reading the speaker guidelines and deadlines.

☐ Also, if you do not already know, ask whether continuing education credits are available for those who attend the speech/presentation (CLE, CE, etc.).

☐ If there is no such credit, and you think continuing education credits would be valued by potential attendees, work to arrange credit(s) as appropriate if your firm has the appropriate time and resources.

☐ Email as soon as possible the appropriate marketing or business development personnel within your firm (if available) to let them know about the speaking engagement.

☐ In the email, include all details, links, etc., and ask the personnel to please post as appropriate on the firm's website, intranet, other sites and so forth.

☐ If there are no marketing personnel, be sure your assistant knows about the speaking engagement.

☐ **Post on social media.**

☐ Work with your firm's marketing staff or an outside business development coach to create social media posts and a schedule for social media posts.

☐ As soon as possible, post the speaking engagement on your LinkedIn page and other relevant social media sites, along with a link for registration.

☐ In your social media post(s), write out the event hashtag at the end. Also, tag the names of the event organizers, fellow speakers and/or attendees (e.g., @Julie Savarino).

☐ Be sure to state authentically how appreciative you are of the opportunity to be speaking alongside any other speakers (and tag them in social media as well).

☐ When you tag people, you bring additional views to your post. In addition, when the event organizers see that you are promoting it, they may be more inclined to ask you to future events.

☐ Work with your firm's marketing staff to post on the firm's social media channels before and after the event, with photos if available. If there is video, be sure to share that as well.

☐ Consider issuing a press release. Whether or not the story is picked up, it gets your name in front of media contacts who are associated with topics of expertise.

☐ If a media outlet picks up the piece (it could be a legal news publication, alumni news, etc.), share the post, tag the publication and the key people, and thank them. The outlet will be more likely to pick up a news item about you again in the future if they know you are helping drive views and likes of their posts.

☐ **Inform and/or invite your key contacts.**

☐ As appropriate, consider your key clients, referral sources, champions, and your prospective clients and referral sources, both within the firm and externally.

☐ Would they be interested in knowing about this?

☐ Would they be interested in attending or inviting some of their clients/contacts?

☐ Would they be interested in co-presenting?

☐ If so, email them the information.

☐ **Schedule time to prepare presentation materials.**

☐ If a paper, an article or original materials are required for the speech/presentation:

☐ Consider what you or your colleagues have written or spoken on in the past that is similar or related subject matter to what you have been asked to speak about.

☐ Ask for assistance to compile information and research as needed.

☐ Consider asking another lawyer, referral source or colleague to help in the drafting.

☐ If it is appropriate, suggest that after the speech, the two of you co-author an article using the same material (so that the professional assisting you will gain some credit and exposure as well).

☐ **Plan ahead to provide valuable materials.**

☐ Make sure that your written materials (handouts, articles, etc.) provide information that you might not cover during your speech or presentation, but that attendees will find useful and valuable if they take the time to read it.

☐ Plan to mention this toward the end of your speech or presentation.

☐ Similarly, make sure that the oral remarks you plan to deliver include information over and above what can simply be gained by reading the written materials.

☐ To be memorable, your speech needs to be interesting, informative and compelling to the audience.

☐ **Abide by the Rule of 7.**

> ☐ When creating PowerPoint® slides, remember to use no more than seven bullets listed vertically on any one slide and no more than seven words across any line (known as the "Rule of 7").

> ☐ Plan to elaborate on slide content as you talk.

> ☐ As much substance as possible beyond the summary slide text should be included in the handout – not on the PowerPoint® slides.

> ☐ The greatest mistake lawyers and other professionals make when presenting is that they tend to use their slides as a crutch and simply read them. This generally makes for a dry and unengaging presentation.

☐ **Understand the two main elements of great speeches: substance and delivery.**

> ☐ Assuming your substantive knowledge is solid, make sure you take time to plan ahead (and practice, if possible) for your delivery.

> ☐ At a minimum, ask a colleague, friend or spouse to observe as you practice the first 10 and the last 10 minutes of your speech.

> ☐ Better yet, videotape and watch your presentation.

☐ Use the feedback to improve.

☐ Remember, the world's greatest speakers are made by practicing, practicing and practicing over time. Very, very few people are born as naturally great speakers and presenters.

☐ **Calm and center yourself before speaking.**

☐ There is a reason public speaking is one of the greatest fears people have! It is stressful and nerve-wracking for the vast majority of people.

☐ To minimize fear and anxiety, and to maximize the effectiveness of your delivery, go somewhere quiet about 15 minutes before your speech (bathrooms are great for this, but an empty room or even just a corner will do).

☐ Breathe in and out *slowly*. Perform a five-counts-in/five-counts-out breathing routine *at least* three times.

☐ This will cause a relaxation reflex within you that will help you relax and perform at your best.

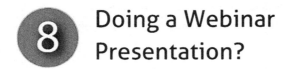 Doing a Webinar
Presentation?

11 Ways to Get the Best Results from Your Time and Effort

☐ **Define your webinar presentation objectives.**

☐ In other words, what results do you want to see from your webinar presentation? If your objective is to get new business opportunities from the webinar, remember that the main hurdle when using webinars to make a strong impression on prospective client attendees is the lack of a real-life, in person, physical connection.

☐ In a webinar format, you are unable to be in the same room and meet attendees in person, one to one, or to shake their hand, make direct eye contact, etc.

☐ This is a hurdle to developing a strong connection because in-person contact is an important factor in most (though not all) decisions to hire outside counsel, advisors and consultants.

☐ Therefore, you may want to plan for ways to insert attendee interaction into your webinar presentation well before you deliver it.

☐ To overcome the lack of in-person, physical contact with webinar attendees, investigate the audience interaction features of the webinar/video-conference system you will be using. Many webinar programs allow the audience to ask questions, chat or answer polling questions. You may want to use one or more of these features to engage your audience and interact with them.

☐ **Consider and plan for the 5 Ps.**

    ☐ Remember: prior preparation prevents poor performance (the 5 Ps). This helps you put your best foot forward.

    ☐ Plan and prepare well ahead of time to make the most out of your webinar performance and to maximize results. Specific preparation suggestions are below.

☐ **Prepare for your use of total webinar time.**

    ☐ Plan at least 30%-40% of your allotted presentation time for questions/comments, but also be prepared so that you have enough useful, relevant content to deliver in case there aren't many questions.

    ☐ Prepare responses to commonly asked questions ahead of time, so that if the audience does not ask any questions, you can state, "I am often asked X, and I suggest Y."

    ☐ Prepare and script "housekeeping" remarks that include what you are going to cover and how the audience can interact with you.

    ☐ Create and send a how-to slide as well, summarizing the exact steps attendees need to take to ask questions or make comments. Title it "Tools You Can Use During This Webinar."

☐ Mention that you welcome questions and comments, and let attendees know the ways they can ask questions or make comments using the appropriate audience interaction feature.

☐ Consider sending to webinar attendees a copy of the slides that you will use before or during the webinar. Send them well ahead of the start time, so attendees can follow along and take notes in the most organized manner that works for them.

☐ If you decide not to send slides ahead of time, be sure to mention that you will be emailing a copy of the slides immediately after the webinar.

☐ **Build "calls to action" into your presentation and/or slides at appropriate points throughout.**

☐ This is especially important at the beginning and the end of your presentation.

☐ A call to action at the beginning of your presentation lets attendees know they can ask questions or make comments, and describes how to do so. A call to action at the end of your presentation can be a slide with a list that offers specific additional materials, a suggested reading list, site links, etc., so attendees can find out more about what was covered.

☐ Be sure to include a slide that contains your contact information – at least your email, phone and LinkedIn page link that invites attendees to "Connect with"/ "Follow" you (and other links as appropriate, such as your Twitter handle, etc.).

☐ You may also want to include a slide that details exactly how to sign up/opt in to your firm's relevant emails (and maybe even provide a list of the various emails/publications your firm distributes).

☐ Encourage the entire audience to contact you in the coming days/weeks if they have additional questions. Include an end slide that says, "Thank you," and includes all your contact information.

☐ **Plan and prepare appropriate social media posts.**

☐ Create a schedule of relevant posts (of appropriate length) for LinkedIn, Twitter and other relevant social media platforms.

☐ Plan ahead to post the webinar on your LinkedIn page and other relevant social media sites, along with a link for registration.

☐ Be sure to include appropriate hashtags at the end of each post, such as #FCPA, #EmploymentLaw, #ERISA, #DivorceLawyer, etc.

☐ With relevant social media post(s), tag the names of the firm, the event organizer(s) and fellow speakers. When you tag people, you bring additional views to your post. Work with your firm's marketing staff to post on the firm' social media channels before and after the webinar, with screenshots, relevant images or photos.

☐ Consider issuing a press release. Whether or not the story is picked up, it gets your name in front of media contacts who are associated with topics of expertise. If a media outlet picks up the piece (it could be a legal news publication, alumni news, etc.), share the post, tag the publication and the key people, and thank them. The outlet will be more likely to pick up a news item about you again in the future if they know you are helping drive views and likes of their posts.

☐ If there is a video link to the webinar once it is over, post that as well.

☐ **Use audience polling.**

☐ Polling the audience is an effective way to insert audience interaction into a webinar and also keep your audience's attention.

☐ If your presentation is a half hour long, use no more than two polling questions.

☐ If your presentation is one hour long, insert an audience polling question every 10 to 20 minutes to break up the pace and retain the audience's attention.

☐ If you have never created, used or responded to the results from audience polling questions, practice several times before you use them during a webinar, so you can avoid fumbles and bumbles.

☐ **Package your content and remarks.**

☐ In terms of the content of your presentation, prepare and package it in chunks, lists or key themes.

☐ Summarize what you are going to cover at the beginning of your remarks, and then summarize what you covered once more at the end. In other words, tell the audience what you are going to tell them; then tell them; and then tell them what you told them.

☐ Make your presentation title and remarks inviting and enticing. For example, do not prepare your slides or plan to discuss "Cybersecurity," which is broad, and not specific. Instead, perhaps package and discuss "Top 5 Cybersecurity Risks for Business Owners."

☐ Do not put more than seven words across and seven lines down on any single slide.

☐ Use colors, graphics and images as appropriate, but make sure to create and use only material you own, not copyrighted material.

☐ **Master your webinar hosting duties ahead of time.**

☐ If you are hosting and/or leading the webinar, make sure to alert your in-house video-conferencing support team of the date and time of the webinar.

☐ Ask them to help you one hour before the actual start time of the webinar to ensure all connections work.

☐ If you will be hosting the webinar using WebEx®, GoToWebinar®, GoToMeeting®, etc., ask your assistant or secretary to check that the system is working at least an hour before the webinar is scheduled to begin.

☐ Be prepared ahead of time for system failures. For example, if the webinar system crashes, have a call-in number ready that can be sent to attendees, which will allow you to verbally complete the webinar.

☐ **Conduct a rehearsal/dry run.**

☐ A few days before the webinar, set up two computers to conduct a test run so you can see exactly how you will look to webinar attendees when speaking in front of your computer or laptop.

☐ Have your chair adjusted so that your face is just slightly below the web/video camera lens. It is always better to look straight toward the camera lens rather than tilting your chin up (which can make you appear haughty or snobbish).

☐ If your head is above the lens, it will also cause you to slouch, and poor posture is not good for any presentation.

☐ To achieve your best webinar appearance, try to keep your head level with the web/video camera at all times, and look straight into the lens. Also, avoid looking at your own image on the screen, because this will cause your eyes to shift back and forth (which could make you appear "shifty").

☐ **Arrive early and log in.**

☐ Arrive in the conference room and/or launch your webinar program at least a half hour before the scheduled start time.

☐ Allow plenty of time to adjust your chair height, ensure proper lighting, close all unnecessary desktop tabs or programs on your computer, clear the area around you and within webcam sight, test the microphone/position of the camera, etc.

☐ Start (and end) the webinar on time, no matter what glitches may have arisen.

☐ **Use these delivery and speech tips.**

  ☐ Keep your rate of speech moderate but not fast. The more technical or detailed your remarks are, the more methodically you may want to deliver them. For practice, consider mimicking your speech pace as you recite the Pledge of Allegiance aloud.

  ☐ Speak clearly and at a volume of at least six or seven (on a scale from one to 10).

  ☐ Avoid speaking in a monotone manner.

  ☐ Increase your volume or inflection to show enthusiasm (e.g., "Welcome to today's webinar!")

  ☐ Choose your words carefully.

What Do You Think of This Book?

PLEASE CONSIDER writing and posting an honest review on Amazon.

If you do so, email Julie@BusDevInc.com to request a free, bonus checklist!

Additional Resources

PLEASE FIND a myriad of additional resources, including relevant articles, videos, webinars on demand, other books, templates and forms, survey results, and hundreds of other resources, on my website here:

www.BusDevInc.com

About the Author

FOR OVER THIRTY YEARS, Julie Savarino has worked with many of the world's leading lawyers, law firms, and professional services firms to help develop client relationships and new business in a focused, authentic, measurable and effective manner. She is an attorney and a client develop and services coach who holds an MBA and a JD and is a licensed attorney.

Clients and colleagues alike describe Julie Savarino as a trusted advisor, idea generator, planner, innovator, process improver, producer, problem solver, collaborator, communicator, and an outstanding speaker, trainer and sales coach.

Read more about clients say here:

www.BusDevInc.com/clients_say

Contact Julie:

Julie@BusDevInc.com

(734) 668-7008

www.BusDevInc.com

Connect with Julie on LinkedIn:
www.LinkedIn.com/in/JulieSavarino

Follow her on Twitter:

@JulieSavarino

If you liked this book, please consider:

> ➢ Buying another paperback or the e-Book version for your entire team or practice group on Amazon.
> ➢ Writing and posting an honest book review on Amazon.
> ➢ Sending your email address to JulieS@BusDevInc.com to be added to the discount list for future books by Julie Savarino.

If you have any questions, comments, or would like to talk, please contact the author, Julie Savarino: Telephone +1 (734) 668-7008, Email Julie@BusDevInc.com, Website www.BusDevInc.com.

Made in the USA
Coppell, TX
09 December 2019